*I kept the lid on all my emotions
and developed cancer.*

*For the benefit of healing, her mental
programming needs to shift into self-compassion
instead of self-judgement.*

*Fear is detrimental to healing. Fear reduces life
force. Fear reduces the immune system. Whatever
affects life force and immune system negatively
is counterproductive to healing.*

*The dark cells of the cancer are toxic.
When cancer has no longer any reason for
existence in the physical body, the toxicity needs to
go somewhere. To me the actual excretion is physical
proof that healing has been fully integrated on all
possible levels when the client reports strongly
smelling urine or night sweats for a few days,
diarrhoea or breaking out in spots.*

*Healing is one continuous mythological journey:
replacing darkness with light.*

For energetic healing it is unimportant where the cancer has manifested or how many parts of the body have been affected. Once the client is embracing the healing process fully, all cancer vanishes, for it no longer has any reason to exist within the person's physique.

In a nutshell, Miranda's healing process involves empowerment through diminishing feelings of guilt and shame and increasing self-esteem, through restoring balance between nurturing and being nurtured, through expressing and verbalising her needs and desires and thereby putting her own needs above anybody else's needs and desires.

'Genetically programmed' often feels hopeless, fait accompli. 'Psychologically programmed' feels hopeful.

Healing is unpredictable. Expect the unexpected. Expect not to fit into any pattern of what is seemingly normal, for nothing is, in healing as well as in life.

healing techniques in detail, I strongly advise you to be careful and not to apply them randomly. It does take years of training and experience to hold a person safe and sane during an often deeply cathartic process of release and healing. My first professional work with people was at the age of thirty, twenty three years ago, when working in a night shelter for the homeless in Groningen, The Netherlands. A lot of experiential water has gone under the bridge since then.

version sees the light of day. For now, dear reader, try and see beyond these discrepancies and take the messages of hope to heart.

The messages are written from the perspective of a person in a healing capacity with years of passive experience, meaning that I have experienced cancer in many shapes and forms during its various stages, but that I have not had cancer myself. Although I do have cancer cells in my body, just like every other human. Will they be triggered into activity? Why in some people and not in others? Again, why this divide? To what extent will they be activated? Where in the body will they manifest to such a level of activity that disease occurs? Let's try and unravel some of these questions.

The proof, that complementary treatments can be of major benefit, is in the pudding, i.e. in the actual real life stories. For that reason the first chapter contains one of these stories as does the final chapter. The chapters in between contain a mixture of theory, philosophy and descriptions of healing techniques, interwoven with concrete examples. The proof is not scientific, but purely proof from a humane level of physical, emotional, mental and spiritual experiences which enhance a feel-good-factor up to the point that all indications of active cancer can have disappeared.

A word of caution: when I describe some of the

choice that I became a healer or prior to that a massage therapist or initially a social worker. Over the years I kept following my heart. Doors kept opening and new opportunities arose, which I wholeheartedly embraced with innate passion and enthusiasm. The result is, that at present, clients travel from all over Western Europe to our home on the banks of River Findhorn in the north of Scotland.

By writing and publishing the following material I wish to give a message of hope to all who have been, are being and who will be affected by cancer, be it directly by contracting the illness themselves or indirectly as carers. By 'carer' I mean anybody who cares for the person with cancer. This can be caring in the physical sense of providing (medical) support to the person in question in either a professional capacity or from personal involvement. This can also be caring in the sense of simply sending the person in question positive thoughts or prayers.

My aim is for this publication to be approached as an introduction to a larger version, i.e. a book about cancer, how I treat it, how to prevent the illness, how to heal it and how a client remains healed. My wish is to launch this shorter version at the Conscious Medicine Conference organised at Easter 2011 at the Findhorn Foundation. In order to reach the deadline I have made some compromises to content and structure. They will be ironed out once the extended

INTRODUCTION

The illness called cancer is rapidly on the increase. It is rare to meet anybody in our western society who does not know someone who has or has had cancer. Of the people who have had the illness, some have 'survived', others have 'passed away'. Why this divide?

This booklet is meant to give a message of hope and reality from the perspective of a practitioner, who has been able to support many people in coming to terms with a period of cancer. Some survived, whilst others passed away. During the last few years, treating clients with (terminal) cancer has become something of a speciality. Not by choice. Neither was it by

CONTENTS

Introduction

Conclusion

*Illness and disease
become an impossibility
when you connect habitually
with your inner source of light*

ISBN: 978-1461054917

CANCER
A HEALER'S PERSPECTIVE

TJITZE DE JONG

Chapter I

FAMKE'S STORY

Famke arrived by plane from Amsterdam with husband Klaas and wheelchair in a rented car. At sixty, she'd been given three months to live and saw the trip as a last ray of hope. If this didn't do the trick, nothing would. He was clinging on for dear life, acting the rock, the supportive one and helped her out of the car.

For me it was a bit of a homecoming. They were from my country of origin, Friesland, speaking Frisian, my native tongue, which is only still spoken by about 250.000 people. For them it brought familiarity abroad, instantly enhancing trust.

Famke had just finished a course of chemo, taken orally. The consultant had warned her that the drug might affect her feet slightly. A perfect example of Dutch understatement. Where she had been walking and cycling kilometres on a practically daily basis up to a month prior to arrival, she was now reduced to a physical wreck. Supported by Klaas and myself on either side, she managed to stumble about half a kilometre, unable to reach the forest, which she would have loved to have enjoyed. Life's quality had vanished. Her physical incapacity restricted any healthy outlet for frustration or anger. Unable to exercise, she experienced a strong reduction in energy flow, hence healing potential. Needless to say, she wore a wig. All in all, Famke portrayed a typical example of the medication's side effects.

The next day during the first session we explored why cancer had entered her body. In her teens she had nursed her mother through a long and painful process of cancer, resulting in her death. Famke had felt ragingly angry towards the illness that had taken her mother away so young. She'd swallowed the emotions though and projected them onto herself. Since then she'd been scared of copying her mother, of getting cancer and dying young after a great deal of suffering.

Is Famke an example of genetically inherited cancer?

Statistics will most likely say so.

I don't.

Internalised anger and the expectation of following in mother's footsteps, therein lies the true cause in my opinion. It is one hundred percent psychologically programmed and not at all in her genes. Whatever is psychologically programmed can be deprogrammed and reprogrammed. What I mean to say is, the root of the disease can be eradicated if Famke is open to receiving and integrating fresh insights and awarenesses, which can turn the negative impact of her programming around into the clarity of understanding past events and their influence on the present. Cancer is then no longer provided with any feeding ground and the client can heal 'miraculously'.

Dear reader, this last paragraph is so important and consequential if comprehended by patients and health care practitioners alike. 'Genetically programmed' often feels hopeless, fait accompli. 'Psychologically programmed' is hopeful.

Famke, in the meantime, poured out her agony whilst sitting opposite me, sobbing and wailing and cursing the phenomenon cancer. Behind her something beautiful appeared. Her mother entered in spirit as a shiny, energetic shape, vague in outline and without physical features.

How do I know at such a moment it's her mum?

Through visual high sense perception I'd noticed how Famke's heart opened further and further, how from the left side of the heart centre a golden coloured energetic cord reached out into space, as if searching for reconciliation with her mother. Did she call on her mother? Did she invite her into the room? Not consciously. But by concentrating on the long-standing issue around mother and her passing, however, the ancestral link became reactivated and both souls reunited, one in the flesh, the other in spirit.

When I revealed mum had entered, I didn't meet disbelief, just deeper crying as if her heart was lovingly being ripped open.

The warmth, the love, the light radiating from mum to daughter was a sight to behold. The shift in energy at such a moment is stunning. However cliched it may sound, love is all there is. The palpable love functions as a cushion for the client to lay down all burdens and the shedding of tears, the wailing voice and physical shaking feel crisis-like. The control stored in physical cells for decades releases. The body can easily shake, shudder, tremor with arms, hands, feet temporarily misshapen, nigh on unable to cope with the surges of healing energies rushing through a physical system that has been habitually shut down. Ten minutes? Twenty? Half an hour? Any length of time the client needs is OK.

For me, it is a clear sign that the real work is happening, that mental and emotional blocks surrender and that its effects directly filter through into the cellular level of the client's physique. All I do at this stage is make sure the person doesn't hurt herself, reassure verbally that she's safe and that there's nothing to worry about and that she'll be cared for and looked after. In this way I support her surrendering process.

After half an hour of work with Famke, she looked so much lighter. Tension around a previously tightened jaw had eased. Her smile broadened. Very matter-of-factly she commented: "Well, that's that, Better out than in."

She lay down on the couch. Because I had figured out an easy and effective way to improve her walking, I initially ignored the cancer, but began working on her legs. My aim was to quickly improve her quality of life, her positivity, her hope, her faith, her connection to Spirit, God, Christ and thereby mobilising her own healing capacities.

Frequently, clients need me to initially kick-start the healing process, after that I need clients' involvement. Healing is a continuous duet between both.

When working on a client's leg, I do not directly work on the physical body, but slightly off it, in the aura. And then again, not in the aura as a whole, but specifically in the various layers, where personality of body, mind, spirit are stored and where physical health, the essence of emotions and patterns of thinking are held.

The first layer, the physical level, is a grid work of fine vibrant lines of energy in blueish grey, directly adjacent to the body. They exist prior to body shaping itself, i.e. the physical body grows into the energetic shape. In order to stimulate communication between field and body the lines need strengthening.

Famke's first layer was normal for somebody going through chemotherapy: brittle with barely any energy flowing through it, hence depleting the body of life force, robbing the body of its healing potential.

Do you realise what I'm hinting at? Medication interferes with the body's own healing potential.

After clearing, charging and strengthening the lines of light, Famke's legs started to twitch involuntarily. Life returned.

The second layer, the emotional level, is spacious and in its healthy state consists of fluid energies in soft pastel colours. Distortions, clouds, reduce energy flow from the higher levels into the physical first level. The colours become darker, where stagnations occur, where emotions are not released. With Famke having just released a lot of clogged up emotions around her mother, the level had increased in vibration, making it more straightforward for me to remove clouds and replace them with vibrant, energy enhancing vibes.

The third layer, the mental level, is another grid work of lines of light, but in yellow. Famke's yellow lines were just as brittle as the ones on the physical level, creating self-debilitating thought forms or images. Maybe the thought form that cancer would kill her as it had her mother? A similar process of clearing, charging and strengthening followed and legs twitched once more.

The fourth layer, the astral level, is again spacious and contains identical pastel colours to the second, just slightly lighter is shade. Energetic blocks are murky coloured, sticky, gooey and slimy and are more stubborn to remove than the fluffy clouds of level two. They can interpenetrate lower levels and even the physical body. Stagnations are a curious mix of energetic residue from previous lifetimes and the present one. It is the central level, the bridge between the individual's personality (levels one, two and three) and divinity (levels five, six and seven). I compare level four with the earth's atmosphere, which occupies the space between physical earth with all its life forms and the time- and spacelessness of the universe in all its infinity.

Famke's field was very clogged and dark. Bit by bit I removed the mucusy substances and replaced darkness with light.

Healing is one continuous mythological journey: replacing darkness with light.

All in all, clearing the four layers of the legs' aura, took no more than quarter of an hour. By that time Famke was able to move her toes and walk unaided. Miracle cure? No way. Common sense combined with extra sensory perception, some simple healing techniques and loving kindness.

That's all.

Do you realise, dear reader, how such a combination of medical approaches can influence the patient's feelgood factor? Just take some time to contemplate how that impacts on family and friends. How do they feel about their relative, their friend and her chances of recovery? How do oncologists, radiologists, surgeons, nurses, G.P.'s feel when a patient walks into hospital or surgery radiating well-being instead of being depleted and pushed about in a wheelchair by a desperate partner? Don't all people, also health carers, prefer to be surrounded by patients bathing in the full radiance of life? How do you imagine such an attitude affects the morale of patient and his social and medical network?

To me this real life example symbolises the way forward in humanity's approach to health care.

Famke's faith in energetic cellular healing was instantly established, supporting her to enter a surrendering process, one of healing's main ingredients. Her hope for improvement and maybe for total healing was instantly restored, providing a positive impetus for the journey ahead. Do you see how a negative spiral downwards can shift within fifteen minutes into a positive spiral upwards?

To hear her talking later on the phone to one of her sons was one of those precious rewards a healer can expect when results are positive.

The second session began by repeating the procedure of the first, but on a much smaller scale. Little work needed doing. The aura had been thoroughly cleared and its impacts on legs and client's walking was remarkable.

The right side of her liver was filled with cancerous tumours.

So much has been described about Famke's history, symptoms and healing. Not a single word has been wasted on the reason for her travelling overseas for sessions, her cancer.

You know what? It is so insignificant really. For

energetic healing it is unimportant where the cancer has manifested or how many parts of the body have been affected. Once the client is fully embracing the healing process, all cancer vanishes, for it no longer has any reason to exist within the person's physique.

One client had cancer in six organs. Three treatments later all scans were clear.

Last year, after a weekend workshop, I found an unknown CD lying on a speaker. Somebody had forgotten it. It was self-produced in a transparent plastic sleeve and gave no indication as to what it contained. I switched it on. Leonard Cohen is a real favourite. The first several songs didn't do that much for me. A few lines of track number ten changed all that:

"I kneel down as somebody who believes"

"And the blessings come down from heaven"

"And for something like a second I am cured"

"And my heart is at ease"

Never did I figure out who left the CD and why. These lyrics hit home like a thunder bolt. I knew instantly, this is how I treat cancer with such amazing results. It is by restoring the connection to Spirit and how that travels down and through the lower levels of the aura into the physical body, that ease and peace are created in the heart.

Just below the diaphragm, around the liver area, Famke held a band of tightness. Liver stores anger. Previous conversations had made me aware of stored anger regarding her mother's illness. One and one make two. In order for tightness to lift, Famke needed to accept the fact that she had anger tucked away, needed to get in touch with it, feel it in all its depth and express it. By engaging with her anger, she could liberate her liver from its imprisonment.

Whilst lying down, I suggested that she reconnect with her mother's disease and deterioration process, with how she had been treated in hospital, with the humiliation and degradation the illness had caused. Once she began to express herself verbally (mental third level), I invited her to breathe more deeply down into her abdomen and to try to make sounds when exhaling. Gradually more sounds escaped. I kept encouraging her to scroll back into her memory and to increase volume. Before long each outbreath turned into a groan, into a full-blown vocal sound, into screams and yells and howls. Her fists clenched. I got her to use them by literally banging on the couch. Step by step, I got her to enter into a state of rage and express it to the point where her body went berserk, totally losing control. Via emotional expression, the second level of her aura cleared.

You see, Famke had been controlling her bodily reactions in order to remain civilised and gain approval by acting appropriately. For balance to be restored, she had to do the exact opposite of control, i.e. act the berserker, let go of control so the mind's grip on the body could be released. She did that well. For about ten minutes the room was mayhem. Feet kicked, fists flayed, voice burst at the seams. The treatment room is quadruply glazed to ensure privacy, so neighbours do not get alarmed and ring the police. At the end of the ten minutes she looked a decade younger, lighter, brighter, with shiny eyes. The tight band around the liver had been loosened in a more radical and time efficient way then any other technique could have accomplished. The cathartic work on levels two and three filtered through to adjacent levels one and four. Brilliant. Time to begin to treat the cancerous areas directly via work on the fifth level.

Fifth level work is fascinating. It is where spiritual surgery takes place. This layer of the aura is a template for the lines of light of the first layer to fit seamlessly into. Where there is space in the fifth level, that is where there are lines of light on the first. I do not perform the surgery. Spirit guides enter my body and use my hands as an instrument. They place my hands where they are needed and basically extend their fingers through mine into the area where they deem surgery is required.

Guides exist on a higher frequency of energy than we humans. They lower their frequency to a certain extent. When the healer raises his frequency, both synchronise and merging can occur. Therefore, it is my task to place my hands on the body of the client where an operation is necessary, to ground strongly and to modulate my breath to that of their energies. They enter through the side of my neck, flow through shoulders, arms, hands and perform surgery. Throughout the procedures, it is my responsibility to maintain this high charge so as not to interfere with their task.

There I sat, hands on Famke's liver area, breathing heavily, at times irregularly, at times stamping my feet to increase grounding and the earth's charge. The most fascinating aspect to me is, when energetically the organ, in this case the liver, is being lifted out of the physical body and floats in the fifth layer right in front of my eyes, for that is where the actual surgery happens. I saw the strands of cancerous cells as a dark web. Famke's cancer was unusual in that it did not manifest as a tumour, but as a spider web of ultra-thin lines. The Dutch call it spinnewebkanker or, literally translated, spider web cancer. Not being localised in one area, it is impossible to target this form of cancer via radiation. Whilst the guides were operating, the strands slowly turned from dark to gold. In a very matter of fact way, I thought: "That can only be a positive sign." and carried on. When the guides decided the work was complete, the organ was ever so gently placed back into its physical surrounds and they withdrew.

In order not to give the client unfounded hope I didn't disclose the observation about the spider web changing colour.

The third and last session was to a large extent similar. Again the strands of dark tissues turned golden and about fifteen minutes prior to finishing I strongly felt as if all cancer had left the body. Again, I did not want to give Famke unfounded hope and therefore didn't mention my observations. Five minutes later though, she opened her eyes, wept and suddenly cried out: "I have the feeling that I am healed, that all cancer has gone." She repeated it twice. I didn't comment.

Together we walked into the sun lounge.

Klaas came out of the bathroom.

And here follows the most amazing piece of energetic healing I have come across.

Famke almost fell into his arms, sobbing and repeating that she felt all clear.

Klaas told his side of the story. As usual he had been sitting on a wooden bench on the banks of River Findhorn during his wife's treatment. About the same time as I sensed her cancer to have vanished, he, several hundred metres apart, released in his own way. Stomach cramps suddenly took the better of him. Within a minute a bout of diarrhoea made him lose physical control of all burdens he had been holding onto during the few years of Famke's illness, whilst he had acted as her rock.

How about that for energy healing and energy transmission? How about that for a husband's dedication? Doesn't that tell you how the near and dear ones of the patient are affected? Who cares for them? Is there enough space within the healthcare system to accommodate their needs? When can that be created and how, I wonder?

Famke rang about ten days after they'd gone back home. Scan results were all clear. She cried and cried on the phone out of sheer gratitude and relief. His voice in the background expressed admiration and awe.

When telling her oncologist how healing had occurred, he simply stated that, as a medical doctor, he had made a vow not to acknowledge treatments and their effects when they couldn't be scientifically proven. A clear statement. Is it a statement which opens the door to cooperation? No. And that is exactly what I wish to see established during future decades.

Chapter II

WHY THIS DIVIDE?

The question with which the first paragraph of the introduction finishes, has puzzled me from the moment I started my journey with cancer. Clarity has gradually been dawning on me and last night's dinner symbolised the divide.

When a person comes for the first time for a series of sessions and stays in our home for B&B, we get to know him/her really well. The degree of openness, receptivity and level of surrender during a treatment can give a clear indication of the inner commitment the person shows to heal fully. When that commitment is lacking or needs a push to get over a hurdle of resistance, or it feels like that person needs more than just my input at that stage, I often invite a 'healed' (ex-)client for dinner.

The healed client shows something to the present client, which I am unable to show, namely, hope in the flesh. From my position I can tell stories of remissions, of so called miracle cures, of stunned oncologists, of clear scans, but to meet a fellow human being, who has been in a similar position, who has overcome all hurdles and who embodies health and vitality once more, is often the ultimate message of hope.

During such an evening questions and answers are fired across the dinner table. There is a frankness of sharing, which is touching to witness. Tears flow frequently. Lights of clarity switch on. Inspiration is ignited. Maybe for the first time the person with cancer is able to express totally all fears and insecurities, all struggles and conflicts within the family, all the well meant but often ever so confusing advice from friends, all intimidation experienced during conversations with consultants within an often equally intimidating institutionalised atmosphere.

And the dinner takes place in a setting, which is miles away from any National Health Service institution. Miles in the literal sense of the word, but also energetically. Personal touches are part of the power of my work. Whereas medical staff follow strict guidelines, procedures and statistical data and treat the client accordingly, a complementary practitioner treats the person holistically. Whereas medical staff are geared up to reducing symptoms, the complementary practitioner aims to support the client in curing the root of the illness: if you pull the top off a weed (remove the symptom) and leave the root, the weed (disease) soon resurfaces and roots keep absorbing nutrition/energy, depleting the intended crop, depleting the person from healing potential. Whereas medical staff have a limited range of treatments available, complementary practitioners can tap into a much wider variety of approaches, including those of the NHS.

Rest assured, dear ones, who work with heart and soul within a medical establishment. Most of you aim for the highest result possible with the well-being of your patients strongly embedded in minds and hearts. You're treasures, valued by the ones you work for and their nearest and dearest.

But, when will the worlds of conventional and complementary healthcare meet in full cooperation for the benefit of humankind? The time is dawning. Patience will be rewarded. Pioneers heading in this direction will be honoured. The resistance within the established medical profession to mutual acceptance is still strong. Many more voices of dissatisfaction are being heard though, from within the institutions and invitations from either side of the spectrum are being extended to also include other perspectives. Therein lies the future. Not in opposing worlds, but in joining the forces of scientific knowledge and experience within the medical world on the one hand and on the other hand the insights and experiences of the world of complementary practitioners.

It is in the joining of both approaches, in full understanding and respect of each other's wisdom, where real progress is possible with regard to the success rate of treatments. By success rate I do not mean, for the patient with cancer to necessarily live longer, but to maintain dignity and retain a high quality of life, including mobility, social interests, hobbies, travel, etc.

Back to the main dinner question of why the divide exists between the one person being capable of healing and the other one apparently not.

The one sails into the house followed by her husband and instantly fills the space with admirable life force. There is a huge aura around her. Her voice is full of gratitude for having been invited and full of enthusiasm about the evening ahead. Husband gets introduced in a flurry of comments and questions. A guy with life in his eyes, who looks at his wife with love and respect. A guy who has been at her side

throughout the journey. Their togetherness is striking.

The other comes down the stairs, carefully, silently, contained in an energy field of protectiveness. Shakes hands and says the right things ever so politely. Eye contact is fleeting. There is a heavy air of resistance about her, as if she is saying: "Why am I having to endure this encounter?"

The placing around the table: both women next to each other. Husband at the head of the table. Partner and me opposite both women.

A bit of general chit-chat about nothing in particular follows, in which both Jacky and husband take part, asking and answering, leaning forward in full participation.

Janice sits and eats with straight spine, silently observing, energy field pulled backwards.

Until suddenly, Jacky turns upper body and attention in her direction and asks: "Tell me your story, Janice. When did you find out you had cancer?" She has left a high flying career in social work behind and is familiar with asking questions.

Janice glances sideways as if caught out, then stares again at her soup bowl. Her reply is filled with trepidation: "Well ..... last autumn I discovered something hard in my breast. It didn't feel like a lump. Just a strand where the tissue was less soft. So, I dismissed it as nothing to worry about."

"The word 'lump' isn't right, you know. It often doesn't feel like a lump. My oncologist admitted that it is a misleading term. But, everybody always calls it a lump. So you dismissed it?"

"I just never thought the illness would affect me."

"And then?"

"Well ....."

It was fascinating to see Jacky in 'my role' as asker and to witness the immense difference in involvement. The one firing on all cylinders. The other dulled.

"..... Then I went to see my G.P. He sent me for a scan. I was diagnosed three months ago."

"What do they plan to do with you?"

"Mastectomy. They gave me a date in two weeks time and afterwards chemo."

"Are you going to go ahead with it?"

"Well ..... I guess I have to. They leave me no choice."

"I had the same, you know, three years back. But I asked for time to make up my mind. They made no fuss about it. And then I took charge and checked whatever else was available. Didn't I, Barry?"

"Yes, she spent hours browsing the web and came up with the most amazing information. Like this one top oncologist in The States saying that chemotherapy should be stopped straight away. That it is way too harsh a method for the body to cope with and that the side effects are so horrendous that people's quality of life disintegrates. And that basically more people die of chemo than it cures."

"True and are you aware, that through simple techniques almost all side effects can be prevented? Many years ago, before I started giving healings, I had a massage practice in Dumfriesshire. A woman asked whether I could help her not getting nauseous after chemo. At that time I hadn't yet learned how to treat cancer, but I knew how to clear clouds and mucus from the aura. We tried it out. She came each time immediately after chemo and each time I cleansed her aura. All side effects vanished. Up to the point that she burst out crying when she realised there was one occasion when I couldn't see her afterwards. Sure enough, she got sick that time."

"Did she not suffer hair loss either?"

"No, nothing like that. If only medical staff would acknowledge our work and begin to integrate it into their programme. Instead of the patient losing energy due to battling side effects, they can use their energy productively for the sake of healing. That's why both approaches need to join forces for the benefit of the whole. Ultimately, clearing the aura is a very simple and cost effective technique. Patients retain their dignity and feel so much more positive about the illness and the treatments. Where there is more positivity, there is more hope, which, in turn, reinforces positivity and the person enters an upward spiral instead of a downward one filled with dread and fear, doom and gloom, which is more often the case."

"Would that work for me?" Janice's voice oozed doubt and disbelief.

"Can't see why not. You're no different than the other woman. Both of you have an aura, an energy field, which chemotherapy will pollute chemically and which can be cleansed afterwards."

"I'd better go for chemo then."

"Have you explored other options?"

"Well ..... I'm here, but I've had four sessions and I do not feel any better. How many did you have?"

"Two, two in one day."

"Was that enough?"

"Scans showed that all black spots in my lungs had gone and my right breast was clear as well. So, yes."

"Why did it work for you in two sessions, but not for me in four?"

Both looked at me.

The answer was crystal clear. How to present it without making Janice feel inadequate in comparison to Jacky, was a different kettle of fish.

"In my experience it has a lot to do with faith and trust and through those, the capacity to surrender. And that, Janice, as far as I know you, is not easy for you. And you're not to blame for that. You've had a tough and rough childhood, where any sense of trust got beaten out of you by the two people you, as a child, ought to have been able to trust more easily than anybody else. Who or what brings you faith?"

"Nobody or nothing, I suppose."

"Thought as much. And you Jacky?"

"I trust that when I do good, good will come back to me, but stronger. And I give thanks for that. Time and time again. Do you give thanks?"

"What for?"

The short and abrupt reply baffled Jacky into silence,

but not for long. Silence was not her style. "For life, beauty, love. Gosh, I have so much to be grateful for

and my biggest source for gratitude sits next to me."
She put her hand on his arm. There was warmth in
both pairs of eyes. "Are you married or do you have a
partner?"

"No."

"But you surely have good friends around you?"

Despite four treatments, this was the first time I saw
Janice displaying emotions of any significance. She
buried her face in both hands, mumbled something
about 'always' and 'alone', sobbed a couple of times,
swallowed and regained composure.

"It's okay to cry, you know. Gosh, I sobbed my eyes
out during these two sessions and I shook. Didn't
I? ......" I nodded."..... My god, for ages I lay there
shaking uncontrollably. My entire body went berserk.
Did you do that? ....." And when Janice shook her
head, "..... I just couldn't stop myself. It all came
pouring out, all at once. And, my God, did I feel
lighter afterwards. As if years of stress with all its
burdens and worries had been lifted off my shoulders
and out of my heart. It felt as if I could draw breath
freely for the first time ever since a situation at work
totally stressed me out several years back. I was
involved in a horrendous situation at work around the
death of a baby in care. A colleague and myself got
the brunt of it, including death threats to my family, to
my kids. My colleague ranted and raved in our office,

happily barged into managers' meetings and escaped on ill health for months to her second home in the Mediterranean. I did exactly the opposite, kept the lid on all my emotions and developed cancer. But, my God, did I let rip in these two sessions here. I learned my lesson."

Let's stop the conversation at this point. Jacky went on to tell about her explorations and initiatives. All in all, her positive attitude towards life, illness, disease and healing proved to be her biggest asset.

Chapter III

PREVENTION

Janice's question, why four healing sessions had not sufficed for her, whilst Jacky had experienced dramatic results in only two treatments, is a key question.

First of all, there is an element of comparison. "If you compare yourself with others, you may become vain and bitter for always there will be greater or lesser people than yourself", states the Desiderata.

Jealousy and envy affect Janice's mindset. Envy creates dark green blobs of sticky, slimy energy in the aura. Such a blob is called energy block. The words say it, the blob blocks energy from flowing freely and where energy flow is restricted, depletion occurs. If the depletion is only of a temporary nature, no measurable effect will follow. If the depletion remains for any length of time or is habitually present, the block affects the lower levels of the aura and ultimately the lowest level, i.e. the physical body. At that stage the first symptoms of illness, be it a common cold or cancer, can be traced. When the person feels the first trace of symptoms, he has two choices: to ignore it or to act on it. Most choose to ignore. Most prefer not to know negativity, but truth has the habit of catching up and overruling ignorance.

The lesson here is, keep the energy field vibrant, strong, cleansed. Basically each illness starts with a disconnection from the individual's essence, its Christ consciousness, its connection to God, Spirit, Universal Law or whatever other name you wish to give the phenomenon of eternal, infinite light. When disconnection occurs, the person loses contact with the divine within, loses sight of the personal and world task of this incarnation, loses the innate capacity to be a bridge of individuation between heaven and earth, where heavenly forces can be manifested into matter onto the earth plane via the soul incarnating into a body of flesh, bone and energy. When this happens, the outer, seventh layer of the aura becomes duller and stops feeding lower levels with divinity and passion, gradually dulling all levels and creating physical disease.

Therefore, it is of vital importance to be involved in life, in interactions, in work and play, in individuation and relationship. It simply keeps the connection alive between divinity and the individual. The more wholeheartedly and inspiredly you allow yourself to engage in this process, the more you enhance your field, your immune system.

Ultimately when people live from their inner source of light, illness and disease become an impossibility.

I invite you to ponder on this sentence. Taste it on the tip of your tongue. Taste it on your lips a thousand fold. Take it into your heart and ponder on it.

Illness and disease become an impossibility when you connect habitually with your inner source of light.

Yesterday and this morning I read eight homework assignments from my 'Bodies of Light' students. During the last six weeks they have started to practise hara aligning for themselves and for their guinea pig clients and they have practised core essence meditations on five consecutive days. They wrote about the effects. Effects were dramatic for many of them. Nausea. Sickness. Throwing up. Diarrhoea.

Embodying the higher frequencies of humanity's

dimensions three (hara alignment) and four (core essence), energetic and physical bodies (dimensions two and one) begin to vibrate more strongly, resulting in the cells of the physical body being unable to hold onto blocks of a lower frequency and hence releasing them.

This to me is the essence of energetic cellular healing.

For these students part of the onset of disease has been removed. For some it may well be true that the initial stage of some form of cancer has been removed.

Then, how do you make and keep your energy field, aura, strong, vibrant, cleansed?

'Love whom you're with, love what you do, love where you live.'

A Rosicrucian pearl of wisdom, which may seem simple in its essence. It is. However, to put it into practice can have and most likely will have less simple consequences. 'Love whom you're with' for example, implies that if you live with a partner whom you don't love (anymore) or who doesn't love you (anymore), something needs to shift. Priorities within the relationship need to change for both involved to return to mutual love or for the relationship to dissolve. Again, I state this in a very simple way. Consequences of the shift can be massively disruptive, upsetting both individuals, their families, their social network, their home, their financial security. Most are scared of these changes and choose the misery of the familiar over the mystery of the unknown and choose for the situation to remain intact, not realising the long-term impact on health and well-being.

Do you know people who remain committed to their partner, whilst knowing full well that loyalty no longer serves them? Or maybe you yourself belong in this category? If so, how does it feel? Do you more often than not feel tired, drained for no reason? Do you lie awake at night? Do you reach for comfort food or comforting drinks? Are 'Strictly Come Dancing' or 'The X-factor' or soaps or premier and champions league your main sources of entertainment? Do you sit opposite each other in silence when dining out? Is your companion a source of fulfilment to you or a filling of space and time for no other reason than habit? The resentment of togetherness creates a disconnection from your (inner) source of light and through that energetic blocks and in time physical discomfort and/or disease may appear.

Pages can be filled with variations on a theme, with striking examples of people staying in a relationship detrimental to their health, of people who lifted their relationship into a new dimension and improved well-being and of people who separated and found a new lease of life or a new spark of inspiration outside of the relationship. These pages will be written, but included in a different publication at a later date.

'Love what you do' and if you don't (anymore), change. Ten years ago you might have felt deeply moved and inspired by the new job and its challenges and how it stretched you. Does that still ring true? If not, are you creating time each week during which you can be involved in activities that are inspiring, that bring you in Spirit, in connection to your inner light? If both time fillers, job and leisure, fail to bring joy and inspiration, what is it that needs changing to rekindle Spirit on a day to day basis? Or has the recent promotion delivered too much of a stretch and have challenges turned into burdens that keep you awake at night? Again, any of these options can create resentment to work, to time off and even to going on holiday. And you know by now how resentment affects your aura, your health.

'Love where you live' and if you don't, move. Have your children flown the nest and house and garden have become too big for the two of you, but do you hold onto them for they are where the kids were raised? Have you always wanted to live in the country, but thought it too expensive or inconvenient? Have you really looked into all possible options, including a camper van or static caravan so you can at least leave the city at weekends? Does your present home fulfil all your needs? And if not, what can you change in- and outside to make it more your own, to make it more into a haven of relaxation? For it is in times of relaxation and enjoyment that your aura can restore itself, release any stagnated energy and be refilled with the fluidity of life.

Please, don't fret, there are many ways in which you can restore your energetic field that involve less dramatic action. Take simple exercise, walk in the woods or on the beach, swim in nature, be intimate, make love, laugh and smile, smudge your aura with sage or cedar, meditate.

One aspect of auric pollution I do wish to emphasise here, which is silenced to a large extent in the media and is largely covered up, is electromagnetic fields and their radiation. Charles Darwin in his 'On the Origin of Species' makes us realise animals' ability to adapt to different circumstances. The ordinary field mouse residing on St. Kilda being a prime example. The furthest outpost of the British Isles was evacuated after a people's vote and government's decision in the Thirties. With the people leaving, the house mouse became extinct. The field mouse thrived, adapted and prospered, weighing double that of his relatives on other islands. Without competition it had food supplies aplenty and thus developed larger ears, back feet and a much longer tail.

People have also adapted over the millennia.

Gradually. Slowly. Erecting themselves from fourleggeds to walking upright is the most striking example. The number of people suffering spinal problems is in my opinion still an effect of physical verticalisation.

During the last century technology has moved on at such a rate that gradual and slow adaptation is out of the question. Mankind is being bombarded with energy currents lower than that of people's auras. The use of electrical equipment for practically anything under the sun undermines the aura's vibrancy.

The last two or three decades have seen a new phenomenon for which we are ill prepared. Radiation from satellites, mobile phones, wi-fi computer systems, electrical substations is unavoidable. In our area people have moved away, because the nearby RAF air base blasts the population with an unseen source of pollution, which creates dizziness and headaches, especially when extra manoeuvres are carried out on the ground and in the air. We can not see the radiation. We can also not avoid it. We live in a society, which is more and more dependent on technology. The pillar of society is no longer the human workforce, but the speed and capacity of information technology.

It is of vital importance for you to sleep at night in a radiation free bedroom, so that your immune system, your energetic buffer zone, your aura, gets the chance to restore itself after having being targeted throughout the day, mostly unbeknown to yourself. My tips: switch off as much electrical equipment as possible and leave nothing on standby; don't use an electrical alarm clock; check the various rooms in your home with a radiation detector and take action where needed.

Allergies are on the increase. Cancer is on the increase. Ignorantly, people are rejoicing at every new so-called breakthrough created in medical laboratories. Ignorantly, people are becoming more alienated from the natural way of being. Ignorantly, people are building more hospitals, for, in failing to take full responsibility for their own health, they are becoming more reliant on professional care.

Is this really the way forward? Does it serve the quality of life? Does it serve people's health and well-being? Is a longer life span a bonus when lived in dependency on medical care and pharmaceutical companies? I don't think so.

Does it serve the shareholders' annual dividend? I do think so.

Is there a place in this publication for such a negatively coloured, political and antagonistic viewpoint? Not really. All I wish to get across is the automatism in which the majority of people live, feel and think, thereby automatically supporting a system that might not be as beneficial as it seems on the surface.

Developing a challenging illness, experiencing a serious accident or coming close to death in another way, can cause people to wake up to a new way of living, to seeing life in a new way and to realise that they have a say, the ultimate say actually, in how to live the rest of their lives. The wake up call can kick somebody into a higher gear of self-responsibility, into starting to think for themselves and planning the future instead of it being mapped out for them. Taking charge brings self-empowerment and a stronger connection with the self and one's faith, trust and spiritual connectedness, resulting in a cleaner, more vibrant auric field, which ultimately strengthens the immune system and prevents further health disruptions.

I'll leave the two J's behind. However, I recommend that you read over the conversation a few more times and check which other aspects you can decipher that may influence the difference in healing opportunities for both women. Check choice of words, body language, level of engagement, openness to the new and unexplored, etc. If you are not yet aware, you'll soon realise that each aspect of behaviour and personality is of importance, not just the physical symptoms we call cancer.

This is as much as I'd like to write about preventing illness, including cancer. So much more can be said.

Chapter IV

HOW DO I TREAT CANCER?

Introductory Phase

Miranda's story is purely fictional, typifying a common initial contact.

"Good afternoon. Sorry to bother you. I am a friend of Angela Dickson, who is one of your students and she told me that you will be able to help me."

"Okay, what can I help you with? ..... First of all, what is your name?"

"Miranda McDonald. Last year I had one breast removed and, after a spell of chemo, I thought I was all clear. At least, that's what they said in hospital. But a few weeks ago I felt some pain again. When I went to my doctor, I didn't see my own because she was too busy. A much younger guy replaced her. That was the first time I met him. He's nice enough though. He sent me to see a specialist as soon as possible. I saw him two weeks ago. A different one than the first one. He wanted me to have a scan as soon as possible. They could fit me in the next day and last week I got the results."

"What were they like, Miranda?"

"It is in my right lung and my liver. They want me to start chemotherapy again and maybe after that, radiotherapy. I find that horrible. I don't want to go through all of that again ..... Angela is a really good friend and she said you can help me. Can you?"

"Maybe. I'll do my very best, but first of all, I need to make it clear, that I can not promise anything ..... and ..... yet, clients have healed from so-called terminal cancer."

"Angela told me that. Amazing. I hope you can do that for me, too. But how long do I have to wait to see you? You must be awfully busy?"

"Yes, I am, but people with cancer never have to be on the waiting list. So I'll see you a.s.a.p. Where do you live, Miranda?"

"Aviemore."

"Okay, that's not far. Great that you don't live abroad. So, if I have a cancellation and I ring you, can you come at short notice?"

"If it fits in with school times or if I can arrange for somebody to look after the kids, it'll work out."

"How old are your children?"

"Twelve and eight, both girls."

"Sounds great. Okay, Miranda, hopefully I'll get a cancellation next week and then I'll ring you first thing, for it would be good to see you sooner rather than later. What's your number?"

"Aviemore ..... I really hope someone cancels. Does it happen often?"

"Most weeks one or two people cancel, so I do hope to see you next week. I'll let you know. For now, it is all I can do, but if you have any questions in the meantime, just give me a call."

An average, initial phone call. It tells me all I need at that stage. A person with cancer who wishes to heal and live. In this example, for her children, if nothing else.

But, and this may sound very impersonal, all details

of Miranda's phone call will be wiped from memory. The only important information is name and number and they've been written on the I.C.O.C list for the forthcoming two weeks. In case of cancellation.

Let's unravel the phone call. It gives an indication of what both client and healer are dealing with via actual speech, but more so via what is not being said.

From the first few sentences, a certain nervousness is apparent. With extra sensory perception I read Miranda's energy field whilst we're talking. Simultaneously, ears pick up any different intonation than a normal, relaxed tone of voice. The person on the other end of the line does not realise how much information she unintentionally gives, which is just as well, otherwise many might become more self-conscious and lose some of their authenticity. And it is authenticity that I'm looking for: their liberated, undefended selves next to the mask of their restricted, defended selves and how both aspects interact.

I observe a thin first chakra, i.e. an insecure connection to the earth, her home in the material, incarnated world. Through an underdeveloped root centre Miranda is unable to receive full nourishment and support from mother earth, which can have an destabilising effect on her position in life, or which can give her the image that she doesn't deserve to inhabit her personal space on earth or in society. She might play small in life. She might be shy.

Miranda's aura holds a ring of tension around her lower abdomen, second chakra area. The chakra related to power and empowerment (in western society mainly translated into money and sexuality) is therefore not fully functioning and unable to vitalise the sexual and reproductive organs with life force enhancing, universal energy.

Slightly higher, the liver area feels black, gooey, mucusy. No wonder, with active cancer. Livers, like other digestive organs, receive universal energy from a soundly spinning third chakra. Hers is clogged, strongly stagnated, indicating low self-esteem, guilt, shame. The sentence "Sorry to bother you" illustrates perfectly how Miranda feels she 'should' not bother me, how she feels in the way, taking up too much space and time, which, in her mindset, can no longer be utilised for others, who might have a higher degree of urgency. Do you feel the comparison? The (self-)judgement? Textbook examples of chakra three issues.

Chakra four, the heart centre, is rotating pretty strongly. However, counter-clockwise, which means Miranda gives out more heart energy (love) than she receives. Mothers habitually give out more love, care, affection than they allow themselves to receive, ignoring their own need for nurture and/or nourishment and thereby depleting inner resources. Cancerous breast tissue illustrates it more directly than any other illness could. Of course, the removed breast was the left one. The left body half contains feminine aspects, like nourishing and nurturing and with that having been unbalanced for at least twelve years (daughter's age) and, most likely, way before that, a left mastectomy is not surprising. A typical example of breaking one of Kahlil Gibran's laws of life: 'You can not share a drink from an empty cup.'

I wonder if any research has been undertaken to establish whether mothers more often develop cancer in the left breast. It wouldn't surprise me if there was a correlation.

How many mothers keep providing whilst running on an empty tank themselves? How many healers? Therapists? Counsellors? Nurses? Doctors? Surgeons?

A band of rigidity keeps her fifth chakra, the throat centre, closed. Or is it the other way around? Have a guess! Creativity, expression and assertiveness have regularly been suppressed. When intentionally tuning into Miranda's throat area, my own jaw muscles tighten. The tension is not mine. In this way kinesthetic High Sense Perception registers the denseness in the client's jaws, indicating years, if not decades, of vocal holding back. Do you notice the correlation, dear reader, between lack of empowerment and fifth chakra issues? Between low self-esteem and fifth chakra issues? Is more clarification required?

In a nutshell, Miranda's healing process involves empowerment through diminishing feelings of guilt and shame and increasing self-esteem, through restoring balance between nurturing and being nurtured, through expressing and verbalising her needs and desires and thereby putting her own needs above anybody else's needs and desires.

That's all.

Sounds pretty simple, doesn't it? Clarifying the correlation between energetic, physical, emotional and mental strands can prove quite a revelation to the client. In the introductory stage, I do not enter such depth. It can be too much too soon for her to handle without me knowing whether a support system is in place for the client to rely on when needed. I purposely leave this to the explorative stage when we meet eye to eye, heart to heart, which, hopefully, will give her a sense of care, safety and protection.

Miranda states, "You will be able to help me."

The verb 'will' dominates, implying an expectation. An expectation of me being her saviour, who'll keep her alive despite cancer spreading. Two aspects are at stake here. Firstly, by Miranda expecting me to heal her, she hands over all power to me instead of claiming her own, ignoring her own role and capacity, disregarding any form of self-healing. As we've been noticing before, the client needs to claim or reclaim her individual sense of power. If I keep up the illusion that I can heal her and that her role is insignificant during the healing process, I involuntarily affirm the decades of Miranda having been programmed into disempowerment.

Secondly, 'Healer, know thyself'. My ego could have a ball being everybody's saviour. Ego would keep the burden of healing on my shoulders, putting me under pressure. Pressure is something I can well do without. It's not good for me and whatever is not good for me is definitely not conducive to clients' healing. In my reply I make sure not to emphasise illness and cancer as the primary cause of her phone call. It can feel intimidating or stigmatising and my aim is to develop a rapport and relationship of equality as soon as possible.

Still, a couple of months ago, when I spoke in front of a group of 'Bodies of Light' students about healing cancer, one of them asked: "What does it feel like to be Messiah?" I protested that I wasn't anybody's Messiah. She simply stated: "You know what I mean". I didn't reply in words. Instead my eyes filled up and I realised the pressure I was under at times.

Unbeknown to myself. And being fully aware of the trap of taking (too much) responsibility for clients and their well-being. And even teaching students not to carry clients' burdens. Student became teacher and teacher became student. Bless her. Bless me. Bless us both.

Back to the telephone conversation.

By asking her name early on in the conversation (and scribbling it down without her realising), I can make the rest of our chat more personal. It can help the client to feel like a person with identity and not just another number on the conveyer belt.

The majority of cancer patients hesitates to ring me and sees my services as a last resort. By waiting until secondary cancer is apparent (or a third, or in one case a fourth occurrence), the time for the healing to integrate into the physical body is reduced. Time is an important factor in the client's perception, especially when consultants convey the message that life expectancy is reduced to months, thereby putting the patient under time pressure, diminishing hope and positivity. It is vitally important never to lose sight of the fact that any kind of cancer can be healed in a split second, regardless of how far advanced it is or how many areas of the body are affected. I made it a policy, however, to see people with cancer a.s.a.p., albeit only for their own peace of mind. They might still need to wait one or two weeks on the 'in case of cancellation' list.

On one occasion a potential client had had cancer for about six years and had known of me for about four of those. She finally found the courage to make contact and was in utter despair when it became apparent that I could not see her immediately. When I did ring her, because a space had opened up, a relative answered the phone. On hearing the reason for the phone call, she informed me that her mother had passed away a week earlier.

Miranda's example reflects reality. Also with her living locally (Aviemore is only fifty kilometres away) and being able to come at short notice, the method is effective for her. For people living further afield, my aim is to have them stay at our home or at least locally for Bed and Breakfast for however long they wish and book daily sessions for that period. It makes travelling long distance more worthwhile and with treatments in quick succession we can achieve a lot in just three or four days, like in Jacky's case. Hers is not fictional.

The Explorative Phase

The chapter's title says it. The phase of exploring commences. Whereas during the previous stage I jotted down nothing but name and number, here a record is being kept of presenting complaint, medical history, client's state of being physically, emotionally, mentally and spiritually. Relevant information is distilled from observation, client's verbal and non-verbal communication, details of healing techniques employed in the session and their impact on the client and finally any homework he might be assigned in order to continue healing in between sessions.

Observation

How does he drive and park? When arriving by car, driving the vehicle and leaving it as if it is the most normal thing to do in a new parking place, can easily indicate a person with a 'wherever I lay my hat, there's my home' kind of attitude, indicating a healthy sense of self-esteem. More often than not this person exits the car and approaches me purposefully with right hand outstretched in a gesture of greeting.

Others hesitate, open the window, asking if its all right to park here. Often it takes them a while to gather all their bits and pieces, especially their courage. Once they get out, I make the first move in their direction with hand outstretched.

Important to make it as easy and non-intimidating as possible to support them over the collection of doorsteps that lie ahead. The doorstep of a strange house. The doorstep of a stranger on whom their life might depend, at least according to their perception. The final doorstep of overcoming procrastination. In short, the doorstep of overcoming nervousness and mostly hand in hand with that, low self-esteem.

The majority of clients make up this category. Any correlation between cancer and self-esteem, be it high or low? Have a guess.

Observations continue throughout.

How does he walk? Some people wish to disappear and not be noticed. Their aura is partly in the room and partly fading into the wall. Beside themselves with not wishing to be where they are. Do they wish to be anywhere at all? Not really. Have a guess how that affects the overall energy field.

How does he sit? Relaxed? Straight-backed? Slouching? Soles of the feet on the floor or tiptoed or not at all touching the carpet? One female client sat with the left ball of her foot on the floor, right knee over the left one and right foot snaked around left ankle. Try that. Can you do it at all? Let alone stay in that position for five, ten, fifteen minutes. Guess how that influences energy flow in the legs, hips, pelvis, sexual organs.

Was it therefore a surprise she wished me to remove

fibroids from her womb?

How does he maintain or avoid eye contact? Casting eyes up or down or sideways with quick glances in my direction easily indicates avoidance of direct contact. Also avoidance of tackling own inner issues (truth, emotions, pain, anger, etc.) directly head-on. Guess how that affects the aura in brightness or dullness with stagnating energy blocks.

This is not meant to be a self-help book. Still, dear reader, I sincerely invite you to ponder the previous observations and make a note of your own body language in similar situations. Why do you react and hold your body the way you do?

Via self-observation you increase self-awareness and insightfulness, stimulating your healing capacity. In addition, it is vital not to undermine your healing capacity by judging any of your actions and reactions. The habits you discover may have served you well and kept you alive and sane in the past. As defensive patterns. As a security blanket.

Once you discover these patterns, ask yourself the questions "Does this habit still serve me? Does it stimulate my energy?" If your answer is negative on both scores, what do you need to change to lower your defences? How can you support yourself in doing so? With which energy enhancing exercises can you replace it?

Let's say for example, you habitually hold your breath or breathe in a shallow manner. Every time you become aware of doing so, you can consciously choose to take a couple of deep breaths. Breaking and replacing unhealthy habits can be that simple.

Increasing awareness and positive intention towards change are the first steps to apply easy and effective ways to move subconsciously held patterns into conscious awareness. Anything you keep hidden, also from yourself in the subconscious, remains secret, implying that it remains a blind spot, which makes it impossible to shift. Self-awareness and insightfulness are key elements on the road to self-empowerment and self-healing.

The healers' role is to support clients in increasing their self-awareness via initially healers' and ultimately clients' own observations.

Client's Verbal Communication

The actual story related by the client cannot be classed as factual. The story, told from the client's perspective, emphasises that which is important to him.

Miranda will, for example, in her roles as mother, wife and homemaker, pay a fair bit of attention to how terrible her disease is for her children. She fails in not caring for them. How terrible also for her husband. Just as well his employer is an understanding guy, because he can almost take as much time off as he needs and so he shoulders her and the children and cooks and cleans and shops. He's a rock. He never complains and is really good at putting on a brave face, but she sees his suffering and how often he takes one or more Paracetamol. She fails in not supporting him. How terrible for her mother, sister, friends who help baby-sitting, cooking, cleaning, shopping. She fails them by not giving anything in return.

The key factor in Miranda's story is the effect she perceives her illness has on her near and dear ones. From her perspective she 'should be' giving, non-demanding and not one-sidedly receiving. Illness manipulates Miranda into the role of recipient, whilst the universal maternal role is that of giver, nurturer, nourisher. An individual conflict of all times, of all cultures.

Is it any wonder she's in conflict with herself? Is it any wonder emotions of guilt, shame, uselessness, low self-esteem play havoc with her state of being? Is it any wonder Miranda judges herself harshly and beats herself up?

It is totally natural for her, mother, wife and home

keeper to feel the way she does. But, does it serve her? No way!

For the benefit of healing, her mental programming needs to shift into self-compassion instead of self-judgement. For her to focus emotionally on her own feelings, the energy field needs to release energetic clouds and mucus to stimulate recovery.

Please read the last two sentences several times. They contain the essence of how illness enters the physical body and how it can be reversed.

Maybe you wonder how such a turnaround can be achieved. Ultimately by helping the person to clarify how one aspect automatically affects all other aspects through the universal law of cause and effect. When Miranda realises the universality of her seemingly individual pattern, she can effortlessly release guilt, shame and burdens. She can effortlessly release self-judgement and increase self-compassion. As a direct result, energetic blocks, stored in the aura for years, decades or lifetimes, disintegrate, chakras clear and are able to absorb more energy. Absorbed into the physical body, they increase energy levels and energy flow, vitality and finally physical health and wellbeing.

Does it sound overly simplistic? Yes? Well, I'm not surprised.

In essence though, this is what healing comes down to. To reach such insights can take some questioning, explaining, clarifying, prodding and probing.

Back to Miranda and how our discussion might have developed. Her first session turned out to be the following week at 16.00. Somebody had cancelled earlier that day. For her, a time when children are home or are returning from school. To ease her into the conversation, I start on familiar ground for the client.

"Did you easily find someone to be with your children?"

"Yes, my next door neighbour. She's got three of her own and takes Beverley and Michael as if they were hers. It's amazing how much she does for me. When I went though chemo last year, she even did the shopping and cooked extra for her family and brought us complete dinners. Soup, pudding and all. Amazing ..... yes, Michelle is amazing. What would I do without her? I offered to pay her, but she wants nothing for it. Why won't she .....?"

Her eyes locked into mine. Questioning, pleading almost. Before that, her eyes were darting all over the place. Practically the only moving body part except her lips. Her hands were clasped together, firmly stuck in between her legs just above the knees, motionless with shoulders and elbows strained.

"If you were in her position, would you support her?"

"Of course I would."

"Would you want to be paid for it?"

"No of course I wouldn't."

"Why would you support her without payment?"

"Well ..... I really like her. We're good friends and we've done a lot of things together over the years."

"Great. Do you think she really likes you too? ..... Stronger still, do you think she loves you?"

Some seconds of silence ensued, allowing Miranda to familiarise herself with what might well be a new, strange concept for her. Would she ever consider the fact that anybody would love her so unconditionally? Would she ever consider the fact that she was loveable? Just imagine the impact of such a novel idea.

"..... You really think so? ..... Yeah, I guess so ..... Hmm ....."

When such an insight dawns and begins to take root, it's important not to interrupt. I allowed Miranda space, time to mull it over, taste it and gradually draw her own conclusions. She swallowed a couple of times. Her heart chakra shifted from a tendency to rotate in a counter-clockwise direction (giving out love) to rotating clockwise (receiving love). The movement was still quite tentative. But a significant change was in the process of being established.

"Does that touch you?"

"Yeah ..... I guess it does. How do you know?"

"Your eyes look a bit moist and your heart chakra, your heart centre is opening. Do you feel it?"

Miranda was receiving outside confirmation of what she might or might not yet consciously perceive and was receiving a mental framework in which to fit a piece of the jigsaw of her energetic healing.

"Gosh ..... Yes, I feel something here."

She rubbed her chest. An indication that mental and emotional counselling was sinking into physical awareness. Time to make a next move in the chess game where there are only winners.

"Brilliant, Miranda, you are feeling your heart centre, your heart chakra. That's good news. Does that mean you see yourself as being loveable?"

"Such a strange thing to ask. Don't know. Never thought about it. Charles loves me. Charles is my husband. Beverley and Michael love me. And ..... yeah ..... I guess Michelle does too."

"They must see something in you that is loveable. Do you love yourself?"

"Another strange question. Well, maybe not strange, but it never crossed my mind ....."

I gave her time and space again.

"Don't know ..... See I never thought about that either. Me loving myself. I can tell you 1001 things I do not love about myself. I never liked my hair. I always wished my nose was smaller. I didn't spend much time with Beverley and Michael when they were growing up. We lived in London at the time, bought a bigger flat and had a massive mortgage. So Charles and I both had to work to make ends meet. My mum looked after the children a lot. She was fine about it, but it was sometimes too much for her. She can't do it now any more. Can't even look after herself anymore. We had to put her into a home two years ago. We considered her moving in with us, but our house is too small. We'd have to build an extension and then we'd be stuck with a massive mortgage again."

"Do you feel guilty about putting your mum into a home?"

"Oh, very."

"Is there anything else you feel guilty about?"

"Oh, yes. Not having spent enough time with

Beverley and Michael when they were younger. I often felt too tired to be there for Charles, especially when he worked such long hours and did a lot of night shifts. You see, when I was pregnant with Beverley, I had to stop working when I was in my third month. A whole pile of complications. Don't know how often he drove me to the hospital, or Michelle did. I must have been an awful burden to them."

"Did you ask them if it was really a burden for them?"

"Well sort of, but they said they happily did it for me."

"Did you believe them?"

"Not really."

"Didn't you believe it, because you didn't know then what you know now, that they loved you? That they still love you? That they see the loveable sides of you that you do not yet see yourself? Or that you don't allow yourself to see yet, partly because you focus on your negative aspects: the events you feel guilty about, the things you judge about yourself?"

"Hmm, can you repeat that? I couldn't grasp all of that at once."

Of course she was unable to put that avalanche into

context. I repeated it slowly, step by step until she understood, after which I asked if she realised how her negative self-image affected her aura, creating energetic blocks.

"Hmm ..... Is that normal?"

"Yes, absolute textbook stuff."

"Gosh. And you can help me with that?"

"I'll try to. And you can help yourself a great deal. You might think at this stage, that I'm not giving you any actual healing for your cancer during this session. But it is important for you to understand how your past has created patterns that reduce your immune system and have activated cancer cells. Together we can hopefully change things around."

"Is that what it's like to treat body, mind and spirit?"

"Bingo. Spot on. Where did you pick that up?"

"Several years ago Michelle and I went to a 'Body Mind Spirit Fair' in Inverness. It was really interesting. We had some Reiki, reflexology and a psychic reading. Fascinating."

Coming to our home was not her first venture into the world of complementary healing. A positive opening. The next step was to give her homework to initiate steps towards self-responsibility, self-empowerment.

The homework would need to be very simple. For the client to play with her new toys of self-awareness, I'd encourage her to become aware of thoughts. Every time she noticed a negative thought or judgement about herself, she was to use the counter phrase: "Hello, old self. Here we are again. Goodbye, old negative self, you no longer serve me." And after that, rephrase the negative judgement into a positive statement. For example, if Miranda's thought was something like: "I shouldn't spend so much time or money on myself.", she could rephrase it with: "Bless me for giving myself all the space I need and deserve in order to heal, so that I can serve friends and family once I'm healthy again."

"You see, Miranda, because you deprive yourself of self-love and receiving love from your near and dear ones, your heart centre becomes empty and unbalanced. Energetically, the heart centre feeds into the breasts. Physically, they're in the same region. In my opinion, that's a major reason why you've developed breast cancer. And .... at the same time, it's not your fault. It'll be how you grew up, how you were brought up and the culture you grew up in. You see? So try not to feel guilty about having cancer. It's only a warning from your body that something in your life needs changing. Do you see that?"

"Yes I do. I'll try and change because I want to see my children grow up ..... And I want to see my grandchildren being born. Do you think it's possible?"

"Can't see why not. I strongly invite you to hold that vision. Go to bed with it and wake up with it day after day. Stay positive and visualise hope and positivity continuously. It can really assist your healing. Everything positive from now on. Shall we discuss your actual cancer .....?"

Miranda had provided me with enough verbal and non-verbal information so as to distil the history of cause and effect. Fortunately, she was open to receiving clarifications. Self-awareness and insightfulness were developing rapidly with a curiosity for more. In a very short space of time a base of trust and client's cooperation had been achieved, making it a very worthwhile fifteen minutes without actual physical healing taking place. Together we had managed to lay the foundation upon which to build Miranda's future healing.

Chapter V

CATHERINE'S STORY

We switch from fiction to fact. Thank you, Miranda, for allowing me to invent you, for you serve a function for tens if not hundreds of thousands of women in a similar position. If you, who read this, belong to this category, please take up the courage to follow Miranda's example for the sake of your health, for the sake of your near and dear ones, but mainly for the sake of your soul.

Catherine was forty-six when she first rang. Two years earlier she had had the first occurrence of bowel cancer removed. Feeling pains again the following year, scans traced cancer in uterus, bladder and colon. Seven months prior to her initial phone call she underwent a second operation: colostomy, hysterectomy and the removal of half of her bladder.

Her situation on the first visit: she had finished chemotherapy three weeks earlier and suffered the full spectrum of side effects, i.e. hair loss, sickness, constant tiredness, loss of hope. The latest scan revealed cancerous growth on the main artery between right kidney and aorta, the right renal artery. Medical prognosis recommended more chemo, otherwise life for her would end within six to nine months.

Such a message leaves the patient little choice and little hope. Janice, introduced earlier, faced a similar fate, which made her conclude: "They leave me no choice."

Does the medical establishment indeed give a choice at such a moment? In days gone by, when a band of raiders ambushed a traveller, the latter was presented with the choice: "Your money or your life." Janice and Catherine represent millions globally who are faced with the so-called choice: "Chemo or your life." Some choice to make. I wonder what percentage make the decision from a fear based approach.

Never have I had to face such a dilemma. Never have I stood at such a crossroads. It is easy therefore for me to ask clients the very simple question: "Are you scared?" Not many answer in the negative.

Fear is detrimental to healing. Fear is an emotion caused by an external threat of some sort. Emotions affect the second level of the aura, as I discussed earlier. If the fearful response is fleeting and threat subsides instantly, the person often takes a deep breath and continues as before. The energetic disruption is cleared and no damage has been done.

Why the deep breath? The fear response is not only emotional, but also physical as an instinctual reaction of our animal self to sense danger. Senses sharpen and through a rush of adrenaline from our adrenal glands, the fight or flight reaction kicks in in order to survive. The physical reaction includes an instant stagnation of breath, a tightening of the diaphragm and a tensing of tendons, ligaments and muscles. The deep breath balances the first instinctive reaction to hold the breath.

The fear a patient experiences during serious illness is simultaneously different and similar. It is different because the threat is not sudden. There is not the adrenal reaction, the instant rush of instinctive need for survival. There is no quick stagnation and release. It is similar because of an outside threat to survival, but the threat is long-term. The threat therefore gets time to settle in the auric field's second layer, creating a stagnation of life force, an energetic block, which in time filters through into the first level of the field and then into the physical body. That is why fear is detrimental to healing.

Fear reduces life force. Fear reduces the immune system. Whatever affects life force and immune system negatively, is counterproductive to healing.

If I talk about clearing levels of the aura in order for the physical body to enable itself to heal, one of the biggies that needs tackling as early as possible is fear. Client's and healer's cooperation is required to unravel it, reduce it and preferably eradicate it fully.

Is that possible, you might wonder? For a person to eradicate fear fully when facing a life and death situation head on? Sure. It's called faith. It's called surrendering. It's called acceptance. It's called serenity. It's called inner peace. Wonderful words and we all know what they mean and we may well see them as states of being to aim for. Sages, gurus, Ghandi, Mandela, Mother Theresa. It's all right for some. But for me, lesser mortal, you may ask?

At a later date I intend to address the topic of internalised images, belief systems, conditioning and their debilitating effects on an individual. Also I wish to discuss attachment to life or whether death is a failure. All that will follow in due course.

How to support a patient, filled with fear, to develop fearlessness? That's not easy to answer. When asking the earlier questions relating to fear, energetic, physical and instinctive responses to fear and their release are visible, noticeable, measurable, hence clear-cut. They are of all times, of all people to a larger or lesser extent. How to measure fear in relation to faith and acceptance of destiny is a totally different ball game. It is a matter of culture, religion, previous experiences, courage and sometimes being faced by the unavoidable and inevitable.

What increases faith on a very practical level is physical improvement, which the client can feel, like with Famke's legs and her regained capacity to walk. Against all odds and against previous messages from health care professionals and statistics, the client realises, 'Improvements can be made and they can even happen to me.' A huge morale boost.

More often than not though, some message or messenger from other realms appears, like Famke's mother. With another client it felt as if St. Francis and his female companion Clara entered. When mentioning this to the client, she burst out crying and said: "I've always wanted to go and live in Assisi." Half a year later she did exactly that. On a different occasion St. Bridget entered to support yet another client. When mentioning this to my client, she whispered: "Bridget is my second name."

Revelations like these bring it home to the person that support can arrive from the most unexpected angles.

When such happenings occur, the energy levels in the treatment room become raised, light increases as if spirit wishes to ensure the client can actually and factually feel its presence, which is more often than not the case. Such a realisation means to clients, that they are worthy of being supported and healed and that help is at hand from beings far more powerful than humans in the flesh. Guess how that affects faith, surrendering, gratitude.

Are such people more special than you, that they are able to feel such a presence and you might not have done so yet? No. They have simply been opened, or rather their field of perception has been opened further through clearing the various layers of the aura and therefore removing certain personality issues. Such stored personality issues can act as a barricade between experience on both human and spiritual levels, enhancing the image that all that exists is what we as humans perceive. Widening perception widens perspective. Widening perception, hence perspective can bring awareness that we as individuals are part of a much larger picture and that struggles on the human plane carry less weight when seen in a more all encompassing light.

Here you have it, dear reader, part of my life's passion is to awaken exactly such an awareness in friends and family, clients and 'Bodies of Light' students.

Where did I leave Catherine? At the very beginning of fear awareness with the question: "Are you scared?"

These three words set inner works in motion. It took five sessions for us both to make sense of past and present, for daughter and wee lassie Catherine to come to terms with childhood physical abuse, for mother and grandmother Catherine to take on board how dynamics between her and the next two generations kept her in a stranglehold, or, in other words, for the woman Catherine to comprehend how stuck her present situation was, wedged in between generations and how therefore the individual Catherine felt lived by three other women without living and breathing space for herself. It didn't take her long to put gained insights into action and create space in her day to day reality, also with regard to her healing approach. She informed her oncologist that she was going to quit chemotherapy for the foreseeable future and her next operation could be cancelled. She went to consult a homeopath who gave her mistletoe injections.

Such a drastic response, dear reader, is not advisable for all those with a serious illness. In some cases it works wonders. In others it can be detrimental.

After the initial verbal and physical therapy work it was clear that the tumour became less active, less black. Still, it was not light. After the sixth session or so the big change came. What initiated it, I do not know. The combination of faith, Catherine's actions with regard to her kin, gradual improvements and healing techniques kindled an inner light, which seeped into the darkness of the tumour, giving it no chance.

And here follows another discovery, which still amazes me each time it happens. The dark cells of the cancer are toxic. When cancer has no longer any reason for existence in the physical body, the toxicity needs to go somewhere. After a series of treatments, clients frequently report symptoms such as diarrhoea, breaking out in spots, strongly smelling urine or night sweats. To me the actual excretion is physical proof that healing has been fully integrated on all possible levels.

I rejoice and congratulate the client with the shit literally hitting the fan. A scan is superfluous really, but proof is so stimulating for client, near and dear ones and, I gladly admit it, for myself.

Catherine sweated profusely for a few days and encountered spells of diarrhoea. She beamed. She looked clear in physical and energetic body. She felt brilliant. She was impossible to shut up.

Her oncologist was of course taken by surprise. What he had never before witnessed on a scan though, was a tumour shrivelling up from the inside out. Radiation and chemotherapy target tumours from the outside in. This time the reverse had taken place, which was a totally new phenomenon to him.

Dear ones, healing is unpredictable. Expect the unexpected. Expect not to fit into any pattern of what is seemingly normal, for nothing is, in healing as well as in life.

CONCLUSION

How many stories can I add from past experience? How many will follow in future? Once other writing projects, among them a fictional trilogy, have been completed, I'll return to this subject and will expand the topic further, much further, including more case studies and a more in-depth description of physical, energetic, psychological and spiritual influences on body, mind and spirit, which result in the development and healing of cancer.

To me the proof is in the pudding. If a client feels life's quality has drastically improved and if a scan reveals cancer has left the body, then that to me is plenty of proof. Proof that whatever journey the client undertook, has ended in a lap of honour, a victory parade worth celebrating. I'm anticipating that in days ahead celebrations will become the norm, sweeping the present doom and gloom scenarios regarding cancer and its prospects from first place. May the day not be long in dawning.

What proof can science add other than confirmation via scan results? The statement from the Dutch oncologist in Famke's story, that he can only take scientifically proven remedies seriously, closes doors, hence reduces opportunities for patients and their healing. Is that what we ultimately aim for, whether working in a private capacity or in a medical institution? Is the way forward really symbolised by the closing of doors and the narrowing down of options? Not in my book.

Without medical intervention Catherine would not have 'survived' her initial spell of cancer. Thank you, from the bottom of my heart, to all who have contributed to her successful jump over the first hurdle. Without complementary therapies Catherine would not have 'survived' the second hurdle.

Dear ones, together conventional and complementary approaches have created a platform upon which Catherine was able to build her own inner foundation for healing the very root of her cancer. The one complements the other for the benefit of the individual patient. That benefit has a knock-on effect as it influences and encourages other individuals and gradually an avalanche of positivity rolls through society, undermining the fear which at present encapsulates the illness called cancer.

The future lies mapped out in the acceptance of cancer as a wake-up call for both individuals and society as a whole to return to a more humane and natural approach, which encompasses all aspects of both cause and cure of cancer.

I invite you to join me in accomplishing exactly this.

ABOUT THE AUTHOR

Tjitze de Jong was born on a farm in Friesland, The Netherlands in 1957. Having been employed in a variety of jobs, of which book trading and authorship were the most significant, he left the commercial sector behind to start a people orientated career by studying social work.

After graduation, at the age of thirty two, he moved to Scotland to join the spiritual community of Findhorn, where life changed radically.

In 1994 he made a conscious choice to become self-employed as a massage therapist. When he came across Barbara Brennan's book 'Hands of Light' and joined an introductory weekend in Denver, Colorado, the next step was an obvious one: to embark on the four year healing course of the Barbara Brennan School of Healing.

As a result the work became more specialised and reputation grew way beyond the British borders especially regarding cancer treatments.

At present he lives and works in a tranquilly located home on the banks of River Findhorn, treating individual clients, focalising weekend workshops and running Tjitze's Energetic Cellular Healing School, which he founded in 2007. Its 'Bodies of Light' programme attracts students from all over Western Europe.

For further information about workshops, personal consultations and Tjitze's Energetic Cellular Healing School (Bodies of Light), please contact:

Tjitze de Jong
Findhorn River Lodge
Newton of Dalvey
Forres
Moray
IV36 2TB
Scotland

Tel: (0044)-1309-674107

tjitzedejong@hotmail.com

www.tjitzedejong.com